TORTURED POET TRILOGY

BOOK I
TORTURED

COPYRIGHT 2024
THOMAS MCGANN
ALL RIGHTS RESERVED

"Except as provided by the Copyright Act no part of this publication may be reproduced, stored in a retrieval system or transmitted in and for or by any means without the prior written permission of the author and the publisher."

Agapi tis Glossas Publishers logo is a registered trademark of Agapi tis Glossas Publishers

ISBN: 978-0-9906241-7-2
LCCN:

Published by Agapi tis Glossas Publishers, USA — 2024

938 Virginia St., # 201, Dunedin, FL 34698

TORTURED POET
Gustave Doré - Dante's Inferno, Plate LXV: Canto XXXI: The Titans and Giants. Public Domain

For Donna

TORTURED POET CHAINED BY SELF DOUBT

Like a piece of ice on a hot stove the poem must ride on its own melting.'

Robert Frost

Well, write poetry, for God's sake, it's the only thing that matters.'

e. e. cummings

"Poetry lifts the veil from the hidden beauty of the world, and makes familiar objects be as if they were not familiar."

Percy Bysshe Shelley

CONTENTS

BE	1
LONELINESS	2
TRA-LA-LA-LA	3
WINE OF LOVE	4
ONE QUIET TAWNY OCTOBER DAY...	5
A SINGLE CUP OF COFFEE	5
HER	6
LOVE LEAPS LIMITS	8
DEATH LAUGHS LAST	9
SOME CREATED REALITY	10
HOW DO I LOVE YOU	10
LOVES MONUMENT	11
FEAR OFFEARS	12
TIME TO	13
DID YOU KNOW	14
PLASTER SMILES	15
ART NOUVEAU	16
ACID TRIP TO HONESTY	16
COME TAKE A CHANCE	17
FRIDAY NIGHT, SUMMER 1946, BELLEROSE, NY	18
HOW DO I LOVE YOU	20
SELF PORTRAIT	21
ANOTHER BEGINNING	21
ODE TO FIRE ISLAND	22
DAD	24
WHO AM I	25
SPOUSES	25
CAN IT BE	26

HAZY MEMORIES	27
TO CUT MY HAIR OR NO	27
A WEARY LOVER	28
LET THIS BE MY TOMBSTONE	29
TILL	29
ONE BEACH ROCK	30
FATHER	31
DINERS	35
I LIE AWAKE	36
OCCASSIONALLY	37
BACKYARD BARBEQUE	37
THE START OF THE END	39
ROOSTING CHICKENS	39
DAYS END	39
YOUR FACE IS MY MEMORIES TARGET	41
MELANCHOLIA	41
WEARING BLINDERS	43
I HAVE ALWAYS BEEN ABLE	44
WHAT'S YOUR NAME	45
JUST CARRY ON	47
KNOWING WHERE WE BELONG	47
MY RESEVOUR OF LOVE	48
SOME SCRUFFY VAGABOND	48
EMOTION S COMMOTION	49
HOW DO YOU FALL OUT OF LOVE	50
SILENCE	51
THE EDGE OF UNHAPPINESS	52
THE FIFTIES	53
JUST ASK ME	54
"SIR"	54
EVEN JUST A SHIRT	56

I HAVE NO CENTS OF MONEY'S WORTH..............56
I AM THE WORLD'S SADDEST CLOWN.................57
WE LOOK FOR LOVE..................................58
A CRY I CAN BARELY HEAR...........................59
OF MAZES..60
EMPTY...61
UNDEFINED FEELINGS................................61
A BOOK YOU BOUGHT.................................62
PICK UP NO RIFLES.................................63
SO PRETTY A CHEEK.................................64
DO YOU EVER DO THIS...............................65
FIRST HINTS OF YOU................................66
I TAUGHT YOU......................................66
YESTERDAY TODAY...................................67
PEACEFUL ENOUGH FOR NOW...........................68
PRETTY LITTLE THING...............................68
STAR DASH...69
COMFORT IS NOT THE FOOD OF CREATION.....70
WRITTEN WORDS.....................................71
AH QUESTIONS!.....................................71
BE RECKLESS.......................................72
DO NOT WALK SO FAST...............................73
MY MIND GIVES ME NO REST..........................73
BOX OF PINS.......................................74
WE ARE ALWAYS ALL ALONE...........................75
AN ALPHABET OF LOVE...............................76
I DO NOTHING HALFWAY..............................76
EIGHTEEN GOING ON THIRTY..........................77
FIRST LIGHT OFDAY.................................77
TO PUCCINI IN THANKS..............................48
THERE IS SO MUCH TO TELL.........................79

SOLITUDE..80
RINGS LEFT BEHIND....................................80
FOR MY SAD FRIEND....................................81
CHASED AWAY..82
UNSPOKEN GRATITUDE................................83
ONCE BEYOND THE ALL...............................83
A GLANCE AND A CHAIR..............................84
COUNTY FAIR...85

PREFACE

Poetry is my first true love when it comes to writing. When I first sat down to write, without knowing what I was about to do, I wrote a poem.

Poetry has haunted me down adulthood in spite of all attempts at escape. Who am I kidding? I never wanted to escape, nor did I make any attempts to do so. While I had a head full of ideas I thought important enough to write about poetry snuck up behind me and bit me on the neck. I was not sure what had happened, but I became a Dracula up late at night feeding on life with a pen inked with blood.

My brain spun on its axis and nearly swooned with the surprise of it all. I laughed out loud, started writing and life has never been the same since. Engineering degree in hand, what did I know of words?

Quite a bit it seems—a talent that would not shut up. A life gift I had once failed to unwrap could no longer remain still. I heard noises like music floating in from near silence. They were words, words strung together playing melodies. I wrote them down and fell in love.

I have written hundreds of poems over the course of my writing life. Of those I have collected some for publication, dividing them into three editions each of which defines a segment of my poetic life.

This, the first book, contains the poems I wrote when I first started writing, from 1963 until 1973 when I left Fire Island, NY and dedicated myself to a more serious pursuit of poetry, and later, prose.

Book II contains poetry written during 1973 when I was suffering from a well-deserved broken heart. I would often write four, five, or more poems a day, volcanic spewings of emotions I barely understood.

    Book III contains poems from 1974 until 2024.

    I purposely elected to keep the poems in as close to the order in which they were written so that the course of my journey would, perhaps, be observable. However, too many poems have no chronological order because they are undated. When moved to write I would grab whatever I needed. Many poems were written on snips of paper from whatever source was available at that moment, torn paper bags, backs of receipts, on backs of discarded envelops. In retrospect I often could not discern where in the chronology they belong, but here they are.

BE

Each compromise is a loss
Each hate is an eruption of life
Each obedience is a shackle
Each sneer a free laugh
When you dope it, man, swing
When you throw the ball, hurl it
When you drink, drunk it, puke it
When you want, lust it
When you love, cry it
Give and be hurt and give again
Hurt more, give more
Hurt more and give more for it
Hurting
Bleeding
Crying

You feel
Live
Breathe
Be!

∞∞∞∞

LONELINESS

What is loneliness?

Loneliness is a hungerless stomach
Is a wanting
An inside crying
A fear
A desperate search
Is love lacking

Loneliness is a sick smile
Is a half-hearted enthusiasm
Is a sensitiveness

Loneliness is not aloneness
Is not external
Is lack of self

∞∞∞∞∞∞

TRA-LA-LA-LA-LA
(A Christmas Poem)

Oh holist of nights!
It is the season, the reason for the season
Lotsa good will towards men!
Roasting chestnuts and boughs of holly
Three cheers for good old J.C.

Oh God grant this night may bring
Peace, good will and understanding
You'd better watch out, it's smart you'd better be
'Cause if you don't, man, he'll pass ya right by
And lay that loot at some other cat's pad.

May god leave me money I ain't earned
A clean hypodermic needle (with extras)
Wipe out that daggo family and those micks down the block too
Who knows what next they plan to do

Oh god grant this night may keep
Those goddamn pollacks from moving onto our street
You'd better watch out, it's smart you'd better be
"Cause if you don't man

I'm tellin' ya
He'll pass ya by
Good ole Saint Nick,
You know, that Santa guy,
He'll pass ya right by

Oh holiest of nights, this night
It is the season, this season
Good will towards men today

And all that bullshit jazz
Three cheers for good old J.C.

∞∞∞

WINE OF LOVE

Love sowed its seed in hope of rich harvest
A bud of childhood, your youth's dying claim
Plucked in ripe fullness at time's behest
To hang trellised now on a young woman's frame

I press gently this fruit between my warm feelings
Then drink of your essence, fruit of love's wine
Intoxicated senses soon reeling

My love for you, life's sweetest wine

∞∞∞∞

ONE QUIET TAWNY OCTOBER DAY

Splinters of light fracture my brain
Piercing the clouds on this wondrous day
Wind ripped clouds track the sky
Each wisp exactly in its place

∞∞∞∞

A SINGLE CUP OF COFFEE

Will I always be fixing only one cup of coffee
Always just one, never any differently
Will there never be two cups side by side I dream
Mine black and yours with cream

How sad I am as I ponder this fate
To think that perhaps it's forever too late
For eyes to meet over two brims daily
As together we enjoy two cups of coffee
So I drink up my brew, bitter and hot
Lost in these thoughts as often as not
Hoping against hope that someday I'll find

Another cup to share my daily grind

∞∞∞

HER

Her
A pretty face, a shining smile
A thoughtful nod, a selfless reassurance

What Is she?
She is me

A positive negative
A negative positive
A surprising familiarness
A familiar surprise

She is needed need
And she is there
She is head-shakingly, incredulously there
As if she has always been there
As if she were meant to be there

She is

Eyes
Not the stabbing brilliance of the diamond
But the azure star sapphire

Hair
Not the blazing sun
But the softly honeyed autumn leaves blown skitterish

Body
Not Rubenesque, not Olive Oyl
But the pleasurable juxtaposition of the always new and time-worn chase of men

She is a puzzle to the unbridled soaring self
The answer to the unasked question
The grail that ends the search that had not asked to end
Yet knew it must
And did not know how
Or where
But mostly why

And the soaring self beats its wings ever harder
Ever faster
For the azure star, the skitterish leaves

And as the wings beat ever harder
Ever faster
Self asks
Can this be *HER*

LOVE LEAPS LIMITS

My friend sat and listened
To my sad tale of woe
And his eyes filled to fullness
As mine began to flow

That fullness, his quest
Spoke tomes of love to me
And even as I spoke
Our love quickened deeply

Such is a friend
When asked what that is
Considered time shared
Embedded in each till death is

But these written words
Mark death's hasty call
For it carries this poem
Over time's substanceless wall

For mankind to share
If he's ever so turned
At some time in the future
To read of love never spurned

I hope as he reads this

He can understand
That a friend is love
And love has no end.

∞∞∞

DEATH LAUGHS LAST

Oh how we laughed at death
With death so far away
Mocking death with a rattling laugh
While youthful vigor still held sway

Sometime later, seems like now
We mock still but with a softer sound
Staring at the mocked as the mocked stares back
Hearing our own laughter on the rebound

And then, and then, that then becomes this now
That consecrated moment does arrive
And with the merriest of shrieks
Death carries off its latest prize

∞∞∞

SOME CREATED REALITY

In the sitting room of my mind
I find a world of relativity
Perhaps a creation of my imagination
Built on hope and love
The fearful drums of my heart beat loudly
Fastened together by the glue of idealism
Living in some distant tomorrow
Where I see it can and will
All be okay

Maybe

∞∞∞

HOW I DO LOVE YOU

How I do love you
Is beyond measure
Yet
Without measure
A love
As vast the dusty corners of a galaxy
As subtle as the humor in these poems
As tall as a sequoia
As minute as the answers my love receives
As fierce as fire

As gentle as your touch
As virile as my hope
As fragile as my life
As certain as my death
As confusing as eternity
As welcome as Spring
As foreign as hate
How I do love you
Can clearly be seen
When reflected by the mirror of your love
For me

∞∞∞∞

LOVES MONUMENT

Such a monument to you
This love
I wonder could you ever comprehend it
Its worth
Though it may appear valueless
To you
In the empty field of your existence
It stands
Unsung, unappreciated
Like all such monuments

As I sit today

Appreciating what I've built for you
Stowing my tools
Preparing to move on
So some other field
To build another
Perhaps
Perhaps not
Leaving my monument
To stand
Forever
In time's memory
For all to view
As they travel life's road.
A monument of my love for you.

∞∞∞∞

FEAR OF FEARS

I stood alone
A world of one
Facing the fear of my fears
Which slithered close, then closer still
Raising its hooded hissing head
Which shook the whole of my soul
I stood facing that swaying foe alone
But instead of quaking knees and rattling bones

I find a shaking, insane me
Laughing with surprising absurdity
At this wispy creation of fear itself
Which vanished with but a single puff
Of my belief in me myself
I searched beyond
For that fear but found it not
It had fled so far so fast
I wondered had it ever been or not

∞∞∞∞

TIME TO

Time
Time to rise
Time to go
Time to sleep
Time to die
Time
Tries sealing us all
Within its own unformed dimensions
Trying to make us believe its limits are our destiny
Few dare try
Still fewer do
Wrest swift life from that hard-clutching grasp

But, ah, those who do
Who do unbend the bent
Conceive the unconceived
Replenish the unreplenishable
Find time in a fury
Stalking them down
Twisting alleyways
Intent on affixing mediocrity
Slashing with swords to instill fear
But...
Helping hand clasping helping hand
Boosting boosts
Laughter overcoming tears
Defeat the slow pursuer
With constant reaffirmations
Of its eggshell fragility

∞∞∞∞

DID YOU KNOW

Did you know
You left a lump on my memory
That catches my wandering mind
Rippling my feelings
As the waters of my life move on
Did you know you could cause such turbulence

Where waters once passed so quietly

∞∞∞

PLASTER SMILES

Drinks are served up with plaster smiles
The bar noise, sawdust on floors and
overloud laughter
Served up with plaster smiles
We talk of movies, the gossip, the weather
Served up with plaster smiles
I turn to you looking for life and find
Yawns served up with plaster smiles
I want to free you from this domain
But you light your cigarette
Stir your drink
Looking past me
At plaster smiles
The loneliness I see
The emptiness I see
The nothingness I see
Makes me want to shout
To spit
To cry
Life is here
Here is life
What do we need

To shatter forever
Plaster smiles

∞∞∞

ART NOUVEAU

My love of love defeats itself
Lying trampled beneath yesterday's brave banners
I choke on each large chunk of reality
Lodged in the windpipe of my idealism
Till unconscious reflex vomits forth these words
The disgusting stench of illusions bile
A gooey monument of ego which puddles at my feet
Formless art nouveau
I feel gratified at least
Men step carefully around my spew

∞∞∞

ACID TRIP TO HONESTY

Joints and James Taylor
Rapping
Love flowing

Honesty choking throats
Delving through death
Till the chilling question
Utters its frightening answer
And silence overflows the table

But the silence
Like the love
Holds hands with us
Around the table

And our glances do not fall
But rather rise
To meet friend's glances
Where they mingle
Gently,
Stroking each other
Nodding
Yes

∞∞∞∞

COME TAKE A CHANCE

I know you will understand
My frailty, my fragility, my willingness to bear
Whatever the hurt, however terrible or bland

For merely the chance at a love so rare
In a sometimes frightening new land
So come with me
Take a chance on love
On a dare

The hurt that you'll suffer so bottomlessly
deep
Is answered in turn by a soaring beyond high
When you are down seeking unending sleep
Remember flying so high in that limitless
sky
Memories now yours forever to reap
In this well protected new keep

So come with me take a chance on love
Oh so deep

∞∞∞

FRIDAY NIGHT, SUMMER 1946, BELLEROSE, NY

Evening still sun-bright as the streets fill
with children, curb to curb
Young girls, in dresses, play hop-scotch,
jump rope

Oldest boys, in long pants, play stick-ball, and ringolevio
Night starts to grey the day, as chores done, Stoops begin to fill with Dads and Moms
Fireflies blink in the darkening night as the first calls from mothers beckon the youngest to bed
Radio's coverage of Joe Louis defending his heavyweight title
Drifts through the open windows mingling with
Chants of "Red Rover, Red Rover," and "Anyone around my base is it"
Street lights blink on cross-stitching the street with cones of light
Except the one the older boys broke with a rock to keep the vacant lot dark
More cries from up and down the block as mothers tuck in their children one by one
The older boys, some girls, in the vacant lot behind the trees, sneak a smoke, a hidden kiss
Black now, quieter now, children in, radios lower, simply listening to the night, smelling it.

∞∞∞∞

HOW DO I LOVE YOU

How do I love you
Is beyond measure
Yet
Without measure
A love
As vast the distant corners of our galaxy
As subtle as the humor in these poems
As tall as a sequoia
As minute as the answers my love receives
As fierce as fire
As gentle as your touch
As virile as my hope
As fragile as my life
As certain as my death
As confusing as eternity
As welcome as Spring
As foreign as hate
How do I love you
Can clearly be seen
When reflected by the mirror of your love
For me

∞∞∞∞

SELF PORTRAIT

Softly rounded statue, muscles taut hard
down deep
Soft curls of red-brown hair weather vane
for a fickle wind
Clear, cold blue eyes smile from their
wrinkled homes
A nose, a bit too large, hangs over soft lips
that scarcely smile
Surrounded by a wiry. snow-streaked jungle
Camouflage enough for today
While beneath this daily more-tattered robe
Seethes

Me

∞∞∞

ANOTHER BEGINNING

And so I see another beginning
Cursing it for that all too familiar state
Beginnings are only beginnings
Never followed they come always too late
Friendship's flame flickers and then too
soon dies

Now cold, blown out by time's short-
breathed wind
Once fueled by our heart's songs deepest
sighs
Stubbed now beneath heels of rejection
Children's laughter made oldsters soon
chuckle
Filling in the blanks on once blank faces
Till oldster's laughed and soon children
chuckled
Holding hands across once empty spaces

Here comes tomorrow! Grab it before it
disappears
Or will another beginning be shunned by
cold fear?

∞∞∞

ODE TO FIRE ISLAND

Fire Island
Your sun and sand
The wind of your spirit
Beats against weak man's attempt to define
you
While your beauty struggles through the
ugliness

With which we men have scarred your face
The freedom of your soul
Touched depths in mine
Till I respond with free rein
To the stomping, chomping choices I hold
bit in teeth
You are harsh in your judgment
You will not let things just be
You strip away the false, phony façade
Like some acidic elixir
Till we all stand naked
Beneath your noonday sun
On the mirror of your sands
In your summer's winter winnowing wind
We learn to love ourselves
It has been said
Your magic
Comes with the first few grains of sand
That find their way into each stranger's shoe
But I do not believe it
Your magic is here
Only for those who come with laces untied
Sand, like teeth, gnaws
Shake the sand from your shoes
Walk barefoot

Fire Island

I embrace the beauty of your buttressed being
And stand that part of you
As you will have me stand
In the humility of the oneness that I am
Before all the multitudes you have nested
Accepting this gift I give myself
Carried by the washing wind
Over the shining sand
Beneath the shadow-less sun
You provide
Fire Island

∞∞∞

DAD

What a beautiful word is Dad
When spoken by some loving lad
That one word expresses love so vast and deep
Making jealous poets search forever with no sleep
Trying to duplicate what can only be said
By no one except such a loving lad

∞∞∞

WHO AM I

Who am I?
A grain of sand
Packed among millenniums
Lost to the eye
In the glaring whiteness
On the beach of time's humanity

Yes
Slightly rounded here
With sharp edges there
Of a slightly different hue
I am

And this realization of who I am
Lost in all of humility
Is the essential recognition
The true pride
In who I am
Because
I am

∞∞∞∞

SPOUSES

Heavy, worn, tired feet
Falling faultlessly in friendly spaces

Find beaten, brown limp flannel
Lying loose over listless legs

Tired, worn eyes
Accept beaten brown limp hands
Across miles of years
Still smiling

∞∞∞

CAN IT BE

I have been told I drain your soul
I burn your feelings leaving ashes cold
I have been told I empty your well
I drink up your feelings till there's little left
to tell

Yet I remember pleasant touch
Which we seemed to like so much
I remember heartfelt talks
On the lonely beaches we did walk

Can it be my heart's so numb
I cannot feel feelings frozen
Can it be my mind's so weak
I cannot recall how our hearts once did
speak

∞∞∞

HAZY MEMORIES

Hazy memories dull my pain
As enemy time whispers sugar-coated lies in
my ear
Till I can no longer distinguish the truth
Each day my memories of you
Slip away
Slip
Away
As I dash frantically after their substance
Finding only shadows
Of already hazy memories

∞∞∞

TO CUT MY HAIR OR NO

To cut my hair or no
To smile or to pout
Blue shirt or white
Picnic or dine out
Rain or shine
Happy or sad
One me or two me
Beyond me

Not knowing
Me
Beating the rushes
In ever increasing circles
Looking for me
Fearing the real me
Missing

∞∞∞

A WEARY LOVER

I am beat
Drained
Empty but contented
Rebuilding my giving heart again
Each gift of love given to its depths
Another gulp of life to the gasping given
Enabling yet another
Giving journey to cosmic corners
In a curving universe
So I rest my weary pen
Tongue of my weary heart
Gulping new life
Replenishing my love
To give to you again

∞∞∞

LET THIS BE MY TOMBSTONE

Let this be my tombstone
Upon which men can gaze at will
In selfish contemplation of each man's worth
In speculation on their time
I scatter these words like ashes
With the wind
Fertilization for each future's future
Regeneration for incarnation's system
Needing no eternally etched marble
Only these brief words
On this flimsy sheet
Tombstone enough for me.

∞∞∞

TILL

Beneath our scorched thirsting dryness
Beneath the lipstick laughter
Beneath beneath
Is
The soft furry warmth of our common home
The warmth to blanket life's fierce chill
With liquid drops of love

Enough to slake eternal thirsts
While we beat trapped beneath our weak
frightened selves
Whose staccato tripping hammer-blows
Signal life's protective sentry
Shutting that as yet unfound door
Till some more desperate tomorrow.

∞∞∞

ONE BEACH ROCK

Held firm by nature's universal glue
In the fierceness of my questing stare
I find before me one drop of life's
immenseness
In this some ten-square centimeter rounded
stone
A speckled salt and pepper rock
Smudged with the brown of nature's irony
Flattened through the ages by an elemental
sculptor
Resembling every deflated, battered ego
Crushed in its time by misunderstandings
I kiss you with my soft fingers
As you yield your reservoir of cool strength
Leaving me in wonder

FATHER

I

Came the time I remember you first being there
A bigness with warmth and affection to spare
A gentleness unruffled, an ear to hear
A love unquestioning, with time to care

Came the time for my first tottering step toward life
Two strong arms did catch and enfold me
Came the time for that message of laughable strife
You swallowed and hesitated but, finally, you told me

Came the time when cruel love crushed my hardened pride
You sat and you listened and then spoke small words
Came the time when my mind could just not comply
With even your rules, still you listened and heard

Came the time when travelling beckoned my rust
You stood and helped pack up all my gear
Came the time when I lusted panting lust
You sat with deep trust, never voicing a fear

Came the time for lost tears finally well spent
Those strong arms caressed and held me so tightly
Came the time I rebelled with such furious intent
You smiled and trusted your values quite rightly

Came the time you stood for my god and my country
But always with such gentle assurance
Came the time I need question each premise forthrightly
You bent with my whims and expressed no abhorrence

II

You taught me of hope
Yet it stabs me with suffering
You taught me to learn
Then watched sadly my differing

You taught me of love
But I live with the hurt
You taught me of warmth
But I found only cold earth

You taught me of faith
But I walked out on your god
You taught me of trust
But the world comes on hard

You taught me of good
While I explored all the others
You taught me of peace
But turmoil's my brother

You taught me of simplicity
But I cast it aside
You taught me of happiness
But mine quickly died

So you sat through the strife
With quiet undriven
Knowing I must be all that I must
Trusting the depth of the love you have given

III
Comes the time I remember these things

With a knowledge exploding and gasping anew
This peace that all you have left for me brings
Knowing in who I am, I am also you

And the things you have taught me
The big and the small, sublime and mundane
I learned from them all to be open and free
To rejoice in the embrace of life's petty game

For awareness has come with all of the tears
Folding your wonders into a special blend
That though I've known you differently throughout the years
I accept you in fullness now as my everything's end

So for all you are and have ever been
I stop in my journey with this message of joy
To tell you, my Father, I do comprehend
That you are who are for this now grown up little boy.

∞∞∞

DINERS

A diner is a tired place
With mottled mirrors reflecting each tired face

The air is heavy with blank despair
And even noise cannot fill the air

Everything is plastic and shiny and slick
Even the emotions seem syrupy sick

While I sit to eat and drink my fill
With more than an empty stomach to fill

Soon all that seems tired is dispelled by a thought
As morning's first rays to birth are brought

As man's day starts emptying that diner again
And once more the vast emptiness of life seeps in

Would that I could build a golden temple to life
On the ground where diners try to fill such empty nights

And take all these people and shake them awake
To a cloud or a puddle or even Eve's snake

For when we open our eyes and turn from the mirror
Colors appear with shades that seem clearer

Next time I visit some diner, tired and old
I'll burn it to the ground to start what I foretold

∞∞∞

I LIE AWAKE

I lie awake
My passion growing by the minute
Intense
Then more intense
My ears become my eyes
Transmitting wind into your hurried steps
Anxious
Anticipating
Aroused
Wanting you

∞∞∞

OCCASIONALLY

Occasionally, hands pluck melodies from
isolated strings
Occasionally, hands write singular words of
poetry
Occasionally, hands even touch
Melodies give me ears, words eyes
Ah...
But once...
Love was thrown at me
Like a book
Tossed, offhandedly across some already
forgotten room
That book landed in my lap
Touching me
Bandaging a wounded soul
With sandpapered fingertips
And you never even knew
You never even knew.

∞∞∞

BACKYARD BARBEQUE

Uncle George with hairy paunch hanging
over his flowered Bermudas

Helping Aunt Celia varicose-veined arms
laden with hot dogs, hamburgers and corns on the
cob
A dozen children, here, there, everywhere
Running through the crowd, playing tag, on
swings, fighting
The horseshoe pitching champs taunting the
challengers over swigs from cans of Rheingold
The children's wading pool filled with
splashing drunks, throwing, pulling one another in
The host greeting new comers, smiling,
kissing, hands pumping
Cries erupting from the volleyball game,
score 13 to 8, but no more do-overs
The old folks under the canopy, whispering,
smiling watching, drinking straight whiskey
TV on in the corner, Yanks 3, Chicago 3,
two out, top of the eighth
A well dressed couple, she in hostess gown,
he I white shoes, white belt, blue slacks
Cooing over their daughter, dressed to
match her mother, crying because she's been
splashed by a rowdy drunk
One pale, gaunt casualty, lying flat on his
back, unconscious, they pull him out of the way
Over it all, Murray the K's swinging soiree
blasts from the past.

THE START OF THE END

The start of the end
Of that that could never bend
The start that killed the dying state
And left as its legacy the birth of hate
So twisted, so broken
That time of needs unspoken
But, I guess you need an empty hole to hoe
Before a seedling can begin to grow.

ROOSTING CHICKENS

Have all my chickens come home to roost
Fulfilling my chartered karma
Till perhaps this work done
I await another course already plotted

DAYS END

How many days go by
That we share each other's presence

Yet never see one another

How may days go by
When a needed word goes unspoken
Because we cannot bear the need

How many days go by
When a smile would ease the way
But we fail to take the time

How many days go by
How many more
Before
We
Discover
The grim reaper
Allows no more
For sights
For words
For smiles

How many days will go by
Before we finally realize
Only then
That the days that were for filling
Have now all come to an end

∞∞∞

YOUR FACE IS MY MEMORY'S TARGET

Your face is my memory's target
Each pose shot hole-full by remembered times
Target used in film and fancy
Till your image fades in tumbled confusion
Lost somewhere between the two

∞∞∞

MELANCHOLIA

I sit alone
Trapped by the weather and my own perceptions of comfort
The silvered lines of rain
Beat against my window
Driven by an impatient wind
And I am sad
And lonely
And don't know why

I am filled with an emptiness
A longing for some unknown
A wanting of some quenching
Remembering what makes me sad

Restless even in these thoughts
Wanting to be light and gay
Yet feeling heavy and sluggish

So I sit to write of my melancholy
To define it
To escape it
Yet the answer does not come
And the glowing embers of discontent
Slowly flicker, then burst into flame

It is the remembering
Of all that makes me sad
Of all the potential my life once had
Had I moved in this direction or that
Here a quiet security
There a warm love
The knowledge of potential confounds me

Still plugged into all the wonder
All the drudgery
All the happiness
All the hurt
Till life expires in the final reel
And we sit around some heavenly cocktail party
Discussing our trite lives
With wistful others

WEARING BLINDERS

We are all lost in the myriad complexities of our own minds
We gaze at life through the windows of our eyes
And speak of life through the network of ears and tongues
Sensing this or that
Through the limitations of our receptivity
Digesting what we sense
With the sameness our oneness will only permit
Till our view of life
Becomes unique to us
And we preach our perceptions
To those with whom life surrounds us
Expecting them to see
Expecting them to listen
While we do not take their measure

We shake our heads in disbelief
That they cannot understand
Are they wearing blinders?
Are they short sighted

We ask
Even as our own needs
Our own prejudices
Our own fears
Narrow our own perceptions
Till they ask
Is he wearing blinders?

∞∞∞

I HAVE ALWAYS BEEN ABLE

I have always been able
To make my way
Till this
Would that I could make you mine
I try
Laughter makes you happy
I am a clown
You like adventure
I become a soldier of fortune
You like quiet
I hush the world
You like touching
I'm all fingertips
Yet to no avail
Of all I am able to do
I cannot do that I desire most

Make you mine
Perhaps this knowledge
Like the fortunate fall of Adam and Eve
Is my reward
Yet it does not suffice
I would
Do
All
For your mind to merely touch a memory of me
But nothing helps
And I am not able
For the first time

∞○∞

WHAT'S YOUR NAME?

We sit, each alone
Mere feet apart
Not speaking because we should not speak
Our lives, our worlds apart
One from the other
By social dictates

You raise your glass
Sip
Sigh

Stare at nothing

Occasionally our eyes meet
Like unintroduced strangers
Then dash away ashamed
As though we had touched

I raise my glass
Drain it dry
And rise to leave
As I turn, once more our eyes meet
Paths crossing
Each looking for an answering sign
Which never comes

So I drift away
Our lives having touched only through our eyes
While the whole world hungers for so much more
A hunger for a full meal
Content yet knowing the empty pain will come again
Would that I could scorn or laugh
These dictates to death
Till life comes panting
In expectation of all that could be

∞∞∞

JUST CARRY ON

I stumble as I try to rise above the pain
To begin to live again, to love again
Is there no rest, no time to marshal forces
Between the batterings my weary senses
course
I wish a moment, just a moment
To rest my heart from all its torments
I need a breath-catching-flash to carry on
Yes
Carry on.

∞∞∞

KNOWING WHERE WE BELONG

We shared our lives one summer's night
We spoke to each other softly of our worlds
And laughed
Sharing the excitement of animal passions
But too much frightened you
For the words of our worlds
Were different
Your awareness reached tomorrow with
light speed

And that realization took your hand
And led you to safely
And contentment
Away from me.
I understand

∞∞∞∞

MY RESEVOIR OF LOVE

I write of my hearts great reservoir of love
Daily stalking with purposeful pursuits
Marking time with heart beats
To blow apart dammed feelings
That will wet the world with deluges
For the flowering of forever fields

∞∞∞∞

SOME SCRUFFY VAGABOND

I'm sure I come across as a scruffy
vagabond
And that's okay
I see myself as me
One individual
Striving daily for truth
Vagabonds roam country sides

In search of their own values
Vagabonds search
Knowing one's self and some answers
Will come
Will come

∞∞∞∞

EMOTION COMMOTION

The wind is rising now
Blowing the tops of waves into mist
Throwing our voices at one another
We tend more closely the sheet and the tiller
The noise rising
Wind thundering ear drums
A concert of whistling halyards and singing shrouds

Hike out

Salt spray washes faces
Burns eyes
Slippery hands aching
Struggling to stay afloat

The excitement rising
Rapidly
Motion becoming speed

Racing above slapping waves
Pulses quickened
Smiles creasing pounding hearts

We are lost
The noise
The taste
Breathless at the edge of fear

Quick deep breaths
Eyes touch for just an instant
With answering smiles
An instant that says all

Ready about
Helm's alee
Quick now
Quiet now
Moving slow now
To our berth
Smiling

∞∞∞∞

HOW DO YOU FALL OUT OF LOVE

How do you fall out of love
Without lying to yourself
How do you say it all never mattered

Without selling short your values
How do you say you never really cared
Without reflecting resentment hiding love
How do you forget all that was
Without a total lobotomy
How do you ignore what might have been
Without killing tomorrow
How do you fall out of love
With the only person who ever mattered
How do you make yourself happy
Without her

∞∞∞

SILENCE

Silence

That magic elixir of self discovery
That magic mushroom expanding new horizons
That magic wand torching new lights

Why do we torment ourselves with noise
Why do we confuse our minds with the news
Confused thoughts clanking one against the other

Listen to thoughts in contemplations
Walking paths never trod before

Listen to silence
There's nothing like it
Try it

Shhh....

No words required
Listen closer
What do you hear?
The beautiful music of...

Si-len-ce

∞∞∞∞

THE EDGE OF UNHAPPINESS

Sitting on the edge of unhappiness I find
A greater disappointment in my inability to define
This itch camping in my heart, this unwetted thirst
Which seems so farcical compared to greater hurts
A one-flea-affliction to be quickly flicked aside

By my minds once unfailing ability to decide
But my unhappiness sticks—an undiagnosed lesion
While I sit drinking coffee waiting for the victory of reason.

∞∞∞

THE FIFTIES

Be a jock, grow a long cock
Play football, be a star
Fuck all the cheerleaders,
Customize your father's car
Drink more beer
Drink faster
See who's first to get plastered
So cool, so tough
Better to treat your woman rough
Garrison belts with buckles on the side
Peg-pants and D-As dressing sick pride
Rubbers sticky ooze in back seats of cars
A complete set of values right from the family cookie jar.

∞∞∞

JUST ASK ME

Would you have me rob a bank
Or be a clown, or swim the sea
Would you have me surrender my rank
Or with bare hands fell the mightiest tree
Just ask me

For I will be whatever you want just to please you
I will be what I must just to secure your love
No task, no gesture, no whim can aggrieve me
If it helps me accomplish procuring your love
Just ask me

∞∞∞

"SIR"

You think you're the one, the one who will never ever grow old
Or when age comes some distant tomorrow you will grant it no toehold
Till one morning some young lad calls you "sir" leaving you aghast

Suddenly wrinkles appear that your mind-
blinded-eyes excused in the past
Strands of forever-hair suddenly turn white
and start to retreat
And you realize you are no longer quite that
spry-ready athlete
You run to the mirror asking can this really
be
That I too am growing old, no, no this just
can't be
As the knowledge of aging sinks in upon
yesterday's brain
A light and cheery smiles washes away this
now-new-empty pain
The understanding that comes with age is
worth the snowy hairs
The wisdom and the peace of mind
evaporate most childhood cares
And as I turn to answer that quizzical lad
feeling mighty ancient, wise and tall
To tell him that aging is a gift life eventually
brings to us all
A gift that brings the wonder of constant
changing hues
But, then looking in his eyes, I bite my
tongue.
He hasn't a clue

EVEN JUST A SHIRT

I found today
Quite surprisingly
That I really like the shirt
You had bought me months before
I used to think it terribly styled
Till once I needed to wear it
Suddenly it fit just like
You knew it would
But never mentioned
It is extremely comfortable
I immediately felt at home in it
Do you know me better than I know myself?

I HAVE NO CENTS OF MONEY'S WORTH

I have no sense of money's worth
I do not understand the pence
I merely view with a sense of mirth
Life's frantic inflationary nonsense

Money seems so trivial yet about its axle life revolves
Without first knowing what we need how can any comfort evolve
So we look for the happiness they think money can buy
Till buried with their greenbacks they're still wondering why

All the cars and yachts and diamonds yield no inner peace
Because they do not fulfill what each man's soul unyieldingly seeks
Rather look to the green of living in a rainbow or a fluttering leaf
And worry, always tomorrow, about your monetary grief

Who am I kidding? I wish I knew
As I scratch my nickels together because I have so few

∞∞∞

I AM THE WORLD'S SADDEST CLOWN

I am the world's saddest clown

Trying to turn frowns upside down
I romp and play
With face of twisted clay
Seeking to make the whole world laugh
Cut all our troubles at least in half
And with just a single jolly caprice
I hope to make all hurts cease
To build a new world to behold
Upon the cold ashes of the old
But to begin I must kill memories past
With loud laughter intended to make it last
But through my antics and hearty guffaws
My desperate heart gambols with pain in every pore
I am the saddest clown
My smile a forever frown

∞∞∞

WE LOOK FOR LOVE

We look for love in love
Searching high and low
Yet cannot find its substance
Until our halting steps have let it go

I loved the girl with fragile might
Yet feared the love itself

And could not let the moment be
Till she took away her self

Why do we realize too late
Of love's mysterious and fragile lace
Why do we give away a love so great
Allowing emptiness to take its place

∞∞∞∞

A CRY I CAN BARELY HEAR

The weight of my body shifts onto you
Our skins rub, burn, scorch
Through our sweat our nerves are bare ends
Our eyes wide open, unseeing, our tongues
our torches

I enter you slowly, wetly, hotly
As we groan aloud full of heat
No motion is necessary, our passions
growing
We smile through the hot, oh god is it sweet

And begin love's cradle rocking
Speed seems essential but we know it is not
We love each other slowly, till our bodies
start smacking

Sounding lust's signal, no longer able to
bear the hot

Your cry is my music but I can barely hear
As our love rushes to greet our senses
The breath is gone, the now is here
Filling, filling filling love's complete
answers

We stay as one catching our breaths
I kiss your closed eyes, stroke your dripping
hair
Our sweet scents mingling, our love so
expressed
And so we love, and so we care, and so we
share

∞∞∞

OF MAZES

I feel as though I'm looking at you
Caught in some complex maze I've just
completed
I see you turn one way to unhappiness
looking to be happy
I see you turn another to turmoil looking for
peace

I wish I could
Light the way
And stand at the end
To catch you running quickly into my arms
What happiness that would bring me

∞∞∞

EMPTY

Empty is hollow
Perfume with no odor
Sweets with no taste
Warmth with no heat
Music with no sound
Rainbows with no color
A thing without its essence
Me without you

∞∞∞

UNDEFINED FEELINGS

I come tonight, a poem scratching at my heart
Impatient to find its message, what it would impart

Because my love has gone and taken away
her smile
Leaving baffled love behind traveling alone
time's miles
Her departure gives rise to these clumsy
words
Trying to make sense out of what seems
absurdedly absurd
Once sure of love I spent it carelessly
Now gone I seek it ceaselessly
For any interest I can bring to bear
And store to more carefully share
Budgeting to spend some daily
Building principle faithfully
But the taxman came
To claim the same
And it was gone on to another
So now I sell pencils to recover

∞∞∞

THE BOOK YOU BOUGHT

Reading your inscription
In a book you had bought
Before our love had died
I pressed the words your hands had written
So quickly to my lips I was surprised

I do not let myself
Do such sentimental things
Perhaps because I am afraid
Of the flood of feelings they bring
God, I must have loved you so
To make me act without a thought
Perhaps our love would still be alive
Had I kissed earlier this book you bought

∞∞∞

PICK UP NO RIFLES

To pick up no rifles seems such a simple thing
Think of the peace to the world it would bring
Mankind fearing not his own fellow man
Thinking of them rather as next of kin
Following not each sick ego preaching
This doctrine or that's supposed true teachings
Living within a love with common boundaries
Without nations, or races or religions flounderings
All this can never be they all angrily say

That's much too idealistic for this modern day
Mankind could never begin to harvest such wealth
I sigh, stamp my foot, why not begin with yourself

∞∞∞

SO PRETTY A CHEEK

I reached to stroke your pretty cheek
Allowing my fingers for my heart to speak
But as my hand approached your face
Quite quickly you stole it from its place
That flinch, you said, when I spoke of it
Resulted from your inability to cope with it
Touching, you said, you found hard to take
And I should not be upset at such a slight berate
But I need mention the pain in my heart
The feelings that tore my sore soul apart
For your rebuff though not for me
Mattered because, of course, I blamed me

So remember, my friend, next time touch is around

That touch or glance is where affection
abounds
A sentiment making each moment seem
golden
Even in that moment and for ages unfolding
The now is the answer that happiness seeks
The now in the touch on so pretty a cheek
So next time my hand approaches your face
Bring it closer to find pleasure's sweet place
I promise a smile will wrinkle that cheek
And after more touching you'll earnestly
seek
So if this be worthy of our lives furtive time
If I teach you to touch the fulfillment is
mine

∞∞∞

DO YOU EVER DO THIS

I find myself searching through your words
Piling sentence on remembered sentence
Looking for some balmy phrase to soothe
Sucking hope out of even indifferent nods
Only to pull the bottom thought out once
more
Putting it on top to read all over again
Drowning in the over lapping waves

Looking for any life ring to which my hopes can cling

∞∞∞∞

FIRST HINTS OF YOU

Summer's warmest gentlest perfume
Carried on each Spring zephyr
My messenger from Marathon
Announcing your victorious being
I love you for all you love
You become my summer
Each warm breeze
Sings to the crocus buds of memory
I thought the winter of our parting surely killed
But they stir anew
Each bud birth's pain
I barely bear
Rooted, nostrils aquiver
Spring harvesting memories of you

∞∞∞∞

I TAUGHT YOU

I taught you how to swim

When I could barely swim myself
I taught you of good food and wine
Without the necessary wealth
I taught you passions motions
Without acknowledging your needs
I taught you idealisms reach
Without allowing your intentions
But worst of all I taught you love
Then left you wanting

∞∞∞

YESTERDAY TODAY

The hugging reality of uninterrupted love
And never clumsy words
Inverted jealous time's gritty clock
Making yesterday today

Only the wrinkles on my face
That smiled back at me from my mirror
Brought yesterday nearer
Spoke of mile-less distance
And hour-less time
In that instant

∞∞∞

PEACEFUL ENOUGH FOR NOW

I find I feel peaceful
Peaceful
That is solace
Needing a hot cup of tea
With its calming heat
To carry me beyond today's troubles
While I wonder what will warm me
tomorrow
But do not ask me to be happy
Peaceful is enough for now

∞∞∞

PRETTY LITTLE THING

Pretty little thing
Sitting at the bar
Pretty little thing
I wonder who you really are

Are you of my world
Are you in my phase
Could you be a lover
Could you complete my complex maze

But I must leave you be
Before lusting knowledge

Scars your expectations
And your life falls from its edge

Of secure and warm simplicity
To find a life more full
Yet more terrible in its scope
Of trips with but few rules

So I sense your presence
And while I appreciate your being
I must let you be
Till that time of your heart's seeing

That might demand an explanation
Of a new fullness beginning to burn
But you must be aware and quite certain
That once embarked there is no return.

∞∞∞

STAR DASH

As I sit my mind begins to jog
It trots down old familiar roads
Then past less travelled yet still friendly paths
Picking up speed as it discovers new wonders

Until without a thought it has raced far
beyond the stars
Lost in the building blocks of endless
possibilities
Which tumble before the tired mind's slowly
tiring feat
And comes home to rest breathless in its star
dash
Gulping new life, catching breaths' being
Heart beating with the gasping wonder of
learning
Before it is off again.

∞∞∞

COMFORT IS NOT THE FOOD OF CREATION

Comfort is not the food of creation
Soothing spring sprouts to sleep
Like flames evaporating the essence of
brandy
Wafting it luxurious aroma
While absconding with its intoxicating
essence
As the master soon depends upon the slave
So too comfort enslaves creativity

∞∞∞

WRITTEN WORDS
[For Saint Exupery]

My friendly tea kettle
Whistles me back to reality
Or, perhaps, unreality
Shocking me of time's swift passage
It was but minutes ago
The kettle and my mind
Sat still and cold
Until the heat of written words
Fired the cauldron of my mind
Living within without-boundaries
A complete existence
In your written words!
Oh, to have such power!

∞∞∞

AH QUESTIONS!

Ah, questions!
Minds brimming to its very edges
With questions
Room after room filled with I-wonders
Why is the sky blue

Is a question
Leading down infinite forks
Overflowing questions' vats
Immersed, drowning in interrogatories
Births of possibilities
With impossible answers possible
Emptying the brimming mind
With answerable answers
Driven by the need to invent
Another question
Any question
To remain unanswered
Beaded sweat on wrinkled brows
Fixed gaze through foggy haze
Wonderings' eternal ponderings
Ah, questions

∞∞∞∞

BE RECKLESS

Be reckless
Without caution
Push life to its edges
Teetering on that moment
Before scrambling back beneath a shady tree
Clutching what's been stolen
Telling, of course, everyone

DO NOT WALK SO FAST

Do not walk so fast
You fail to notice eternity
Haste strikes and stays stuck
Caring not to even understand why
Look beyond mere spellings
To analyze nature's own handwriting
Never walk so fast
You fail to read the obvious

MY MIND GIVES ME NO REST

My mind gives me no rest
It does not sleep when I do
So I roll over and turn on the light
Writing these weary thoughts
Pushing as I must
Daring not let the moment pass
Laboring over this work
That is not work at all

BOX OF PINS

I experience the emotions of life
I laugh, and sing and am concerned with others
But everything seems flat and nothing seems rife
With the depths and the fullness I used to discover

My games seem to end before they've begun
And I couldn't care less about the final score
I hurry here I scurry there, forever on the run
Filling empty time with emptinesses galore

My friends seem concerned with their own special cares
Too busy to look up from their own selfish hands
I know I cannot expect them to be aware
Of a pain so sharp I can barely stand

All this because you're gone and your smile warms me no more
You've taken your clothes, your body and your box of pins
And moved to some new home, some new open door

Where a new life awaits you, a new love, a new him

I'm empty now without you and feel half a man
I miss you, My Love, with a missing so real
It is part of my guts, a pain I'll never understand
Because you are gone and our love's coffin is sealed

∞∞∞

WE ARE ALWAYS ALL ALONE

We are always all alone
Even in our desperate reach for each other
Arms outstretched
Hands wide open
Yet shoulders hunched
Afraid
Alive
But only half alive
Awaiting what?

∞∞∞

AN ALPHABET OF LOVE

How do I love there?
Let me spell the ways
A is for Always
B is for Because of who you are
C is for Crucifixion – my life without you
Z is for Zebra because Z is always for zebra
and for the always that I will always love you

∞∞∞

I DO NOTHING HALFWAY

I do nothing halfway
Never have been able to
Had to run a race once
Lost my stomach but ran
Had to carry a load once
Lost my spine but lifted
Had to love a girl once
Lost my heart but loved
Held spineless
Without stomach
Love lost
But holding firm regardless
Doing nothing halfway

EIGHTEEN GOING ON THIRTY

Oh, your battle, Oh, your strife
As men exasperate your life
Eighteen going on thirty you say
With yet thousands of tomorrow's coming
your way
When this all seems too much to bear
Come on around, let me share
For I know you will never buckle
Smile with me now while enjoying life's
chuckles

FIRST LIGHT OF DAY

There is no life to be found in a bar
Just noise and haste and a role to play
So stay by yourself and learn who you are
Welcoming each first light of day.

TO PUCCINI IN THANKS
[For Musetta's Waltz]

A bugler wakens me
Stroking
Undulating forward
Soft gentle rolling rhythms of patterns of smiling softnesses
Transported beyond the now, carrying the past to present, onto tomorrow's future
The marching steps of firm determination
Never to be easy
Around all sharp edges
Steady, steady forward
Edging, edging ever closer
Crashing into flight
Soft humble light
Arms outstretched laughing with breathless soaring
Restored
Being with all
With hope of life and love
With singing pride
Reaffirmed, refined
Triumphant
Weeping in humility

THERE IS SO MUCH TO TELL

There is so much I want to tell you
But we have so little time
Our lives rush past us
Like trains enroute different destinations
We wave at each other
From behind experiences' glass restrictions
During the short passage our eyes share with
each other
Screaming incomprehensible words
Drowned out
By the clicking-clacking wheels of our own
intents
Even if occasionally one word or two
Falls into a drop of silence
To be snatched from dissonant death
By hungry ears to feed still more hungry
minds
Then does our perception,
Like Monsieur Doppler, have its way
Such that if the barest bone
Of an idea
Reaches either one of us
I am rewarded

∞∞∞

SOLITUDE

Solitude is a precious possession
Many of us refuse to own
It teaches
And restores
For tomorrow's tomorrow
What possession could be greater
Than one that renews more than itself

∞∞∞

RINGS LEFT BEHIND

Upon my frequented notebook
Beside my narrow bed
You placed your glass of wine
And it left a ring
I looked at first
With dismay
Upon that careless mark
Till I stopped my wiping hand
As my mind remarked
"This tells one night's complete history
Could it be but read
Had there been a purpose led

To delve inside such a simple thing
As yesterday's wine glass ring."
As I wiped my notebook cover
I laughed at what could no longer be
discovered

FOR MY SAD FRIEND

I search my experiences for some magic
words
To blot the blur from your cresting eyes
A word, at least, to bury your seemingly-
forever hurt
The hurt that daily vaults ever taller walls
Granting no forgetfulness to this must-be
remembered pain
Till one distant day such memories are
folded and stowed in a lockable sideboard
Knowing that the peace we seek comes only
from within
Words are but empty vessels carrying little
solace
Wishing we could steal each other's turmoil
To sell to the nearest pawnbroker
And head to the nearest bar

CHASED AWAY

Winds chase clouds across the mighty sun
Bright pitches of light celebrate its glow
Again that wild wicked wind blows shadows
Of you chased by my lonely heart

My eyes brim full drop their due
As I reinspect my weary heart
For reoccurring bruises
Once purlpled, healed now to yellow

A hollow near a lordly dune
Becomes my fortress from the wind
While shafts of light stab me in my eyes
Blinding my already blinded sight

Then homeward turn with uplifted head
Lighter for what it has learned
And a few light drops of rain
Wash the tear streaks from my cheeks

UNSPOKEN GRATITUDE

Sometimes when I cannot say thank you
Know by semi-smiles, crinkled eyes
And the lack of distant sighs
That all your consideration is not wasted
Some friendly time a thank-you falls out of place
And its absence speaks in its stead
Know, then, by my silence of my unspoken gratitude

∞∞∞

ONCE BEYOND THE ALL

Once when the stars cocked askew
Once when the moon tinted blue
Once is beyond the all
When gifted with such magnificent splendor
For in the once
Comes the all
In life renewed through love
To carry forth to new heights of grandeur
The love created not only once
But for forever

∞∞∞

A GLANCE AND A CHAIR

I looked up last night at a lag in the conversation
And my eyes came to rest on that empty fourth chair
You should be there I thought without hesitation
But it now looked as empty as a bridge game without pairs

As I looked at it sitting quietly there
Holding no weight awaiting its purpose
Never have I seen a loneliness as full as that empty chair
Did on that night as I gazed at its empty surplus

I did a double-take and the chair was still there
As quiet and as still as emptiness dictated
How can a sight so simple and not at all rare
Fill me with such longing, so unsatiated

Only because of my love's continuous blossom
Amidst my unflagging hopes and desires
That someday I will add to our lacking foursome

A bid so unscrupulously tricky
Praying that sinning trick becomes you

∞∞∞∞

COUNTY FAIR

Yesterday a boy set forth
Looking for the County Fair
Cocksure of his direction
Quite enamored by the dare

He'd heard of pretty women
The prizes, purses, and more
The thrills, and chills, and riches
That awaited him galore

He heard the luring music
It came from somewhere up ahead
He quickened his already rapid pace
Anxious visions in his head

Round a bend, the County Fair
Suddenly came into view
Clogging his ears with music
His eyes with colorful hues

A fabric town of peeling paint
Canned laughter and sickly sweet air

Women with spit on their chins
Beckoned him to come near

Reality stopped him still
Rubbed knuckles into his eyes
Could all the sweet promises
Be but other's dead hope's lies

Where do you go when you have gone
To where you thought you'd like to be
Finding not the loud applause
Nor how things were supposed to be

Loud laughter interrupted
His cold panic deep inside
Because that calming chuckling
Was his, he recognized

So raising his coat collar
To protect him from the storms
A man set forth where a boy
Had stood just moments before

∞∞∞∞

SONG LYRIC BONUS

Let's lighten the mood with a song. Here are the lyrics to a song I have written. These lyrics were sparked by the song "We're Not Drunk. We're Just Drinkin'" Lyrics by Mack Allen Smith. Made famous by Albert Collins.

IF IT AIN'T BROKE DON'T FIX IT

All I know my Daddy taught me
And his main lesson to this day haunts me
Had him a guitar of gut and glue
Played just fine till I tuned it true
After that it was never right
But ever after I saw the light
With no britches on my ass
Daddy's switches came hard and fast

That's the day I learned my lesson
It's OK to stop your messin'
Why bother to even risk it
If it ain't broke don't fix it

My Cadillac was runnin' fine
Thought I'd make it to the track on time
Stopped to put some air in my tire
Next thing I know my engine's on fire
I tried to put that fire out

But the gas tank 'sploded sparks all about
Weren't no cow started Chicago's fire
Was just me trying to put some damn air in my tire

That's the day I learned my lesson
It's OK stop your messin'
Why bother to even risk it
If it ain't broke don't fix it

Was diggin' on the bachelor life
Eatin' fast food, stayin' out all night
Till I met this sweet young thing
Next thing I know she wants a ring
Bein' the man I tell her no
So she closes her legs and does a no-show
I wheedle and plea to no avail
Till I cross my fingers and tell her a tale
Now I've got six kids and she gets my pay
Why's it when I had it all, I gave it all away

That's the day I learned my lesson
It's OK stop your messin'
Why bother to even risk it
If it ain't broke don't fix it
Why bother to even risk it
If it ain't broke don't fix it

Thomas McGann is a native NY, Long Islander, a graduate of the U.S. Coast Guard Academy.

Beside a military career that included a tour in Viet Nam, Tom has been involved in several business ventures. In addition, Tom spent ten years digging clams on the Great South Bay and was a house painter for another ten. Other stints include tending bar, waiting tables and driving trucks.

Tom's passion is writing. He has written two fiction novels, two nonfiction books and the "Tortured Poet Trilogy." In addition, he maintains two websites: www.thomasmcgann.com and www.theriddleofriddles.com.

www.ingramcontent.com/pod-product-compliance
Lightning Source LLC
Chambersburg PA
CBHW050113170426
43198CB00014B/2568